# A New True Book

# KOREA

### By Karen Jacobsen

Flag of North Korea

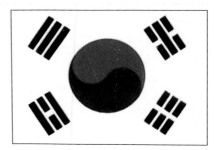

Flag of Republic of Korea

CHILDRENS PRESS®
CHICAGO

Korean child in traditional clothes

PHOTO CREDITS

AP/Wide World Photos—14, 26, 29

© Cameramann International Ltd.—12 (right), 15 (bottom right), 16 (top left), 18, 30 (2 photos), 33 (2 bottom photos), 34 (2 photos), 35 (right), 36 (2 photos), 37, 38, 40, 41 (right), 42 (2 photos), 45

Courtesy Flag Research Center, Winchester, MA 01890—1

The Marilyn Gartman Agency—Brent Winebrenner, 15 (top), 17, 31 (right)

Grolier Incorporated—4 (inset)

Hillstrom Stock Photo—Tom Hanley, 7, 11, 12 (left), 13 (left)

Historical Pictures Service, Chicago—21, 22

Journalism Services, Inc.—Bob MacDonald, 25

Courtesy Korean National Tourism Corporation—6, 13 (right)

© Norma Morrison—15 (bottom left), 16 (top center, top right, bottom center)

© Chip and Rosa Maria de la Cueva Peterson—41 (left)

Photri—4, 9, 29 (inset)

Stock Imagery—8, 32, 43 (2 photos)

Third Coast Stock Source—Bob Smith, 2, 35 (left); Paul H. Henning, 33 (top)

Tony Stone Worldwide-Click/Chicago—Cover; George Mars Cassidy, 31 (left)

UPI/Bettmann Newsphotos—27, 44

Map by Len Meents: 6, 26

Cover — Cheering Korean children

Library of Congress Cataloging-in-Publication Data

Jacobsen, Karen.
    Korea / by Karen Jacobsen.
        p.    cm. — (A New true book)
    Includes index.
    Summary: Introduces the geography, history, people, and culture of the country known as "the land of morning calm."
    ISBN 0-516-01174-X
    1.   Korea—History—Juvenile literature.
[1.   Korea.]   I.   Title.
DS907.4.J33   1989
951.9—dc20
                                        89-10043
                                        CIP
                                        AC

# TABLE OF CONTENTS

Pusan, South Korea

KOREA

# THE LAND

Korea is a rich and beautiful country. It is thousands of years old.

Korea lies on the eastern edge of Asia. It is a peninsula, a piece of land with water on three sides. The Sea of Japan is off its east coast. The Yellow Sea is off its west coast. To its south is the Korea Strait. Japan lies only 125 miles away across the Korea Strait. The countries of China

Wolchulsan Mountain

and the Soviet Union form Korea's northern border.

Korea is almost 700 miles long and more than 300 miles across at its widest point. Mountains cover much of Korea. Low hills and plains stretch along its western and southern coasts.

6

The Songnisan Mountains in South Korea

Halla-san, an inactive volcano, is on Cheju, the largest island off South Korea

Korea has more than 3,000 islands. The largest, Cheju, lies off Korea's southern tip. An inactive volcano, Halla-san, rises 6,398 feet above sea level.

Far to the north, Paektu-san, the highest mountain in Korea, rises 9,003 feet above sea level.

The Han River near Seoul, South Korea

Many fast-flowing streams and rivers run from Korea's mountains down to the sea. Among the greatest rivers are the Yalu, the Tumen, the Han, the Kum, and the Naktong. Their harbors are important centers for trade and shipping.

9

# THE CLIMATE

   Korea is very humid. In the north the temperatures run from -5° F in winter to 70° F in summer. In the south, temperatures run from 35° F in winter to 80° F in summer.

   In most of Korea, the winters are mild, but snow falls in the far north and on the mountains. In summer, heavy rains sometimes cause flooding in the lowlands.

# FISHING AND FARMING

Korean saltwater fishing
boats catch shellfish,
herring, anchovies, and
many other kinds of fish.
They sell fish in Korea and
to other countries.

Fish market at the harbor in Pusan

Korean workers transplant rice seedlings by hand (above) and pick green onions (right).

Korean farmers grow beans, rice, wheat, barley, corn, potatoes, and many vegetables. Fruit crops such as apples, peaches, and plums are also popular. In the south, Korean farmers grow oranges and pineapples.

Songnisan National Park (left)
and Hallyo Waterway (above)

# PEACE AND WAR

Korea is known as the
Land of the Morning Calm.
*Calm* means "peaceful and
quiet." Mornings in Korea
may be quiet, but the history
of Korea is not peaceful.

Korea has had many wars

13

The army of Genghis Khan invaded Korea.

in its 3000-year history.
Sometimes Koreans fought
other Koreans. But, time and
again, the Korean people
had to fight off attacks from
China or Japan.

Korea wanted to be left
alone, but Korea had food
and other things that China
and Japan wanted.

# KOREAN ARTS
# AND CRAFTS

Sometimes, there was peace in Korea. During those times, Korean artists made beautiful paintings and created fine crafts.

Painter (top right) works at Kyongbok Palace in Seoul. Beautiful screens (left) and detailed carvings (above) are found in palaces and temples throughout Korea.

Artist (above) carves the beautiful
fans used in traditional dances.
During the time of the Koryo rulers,
Korean artists developed a new
method of making pottery. The vase
and wine pitcher are examples
of the color and style of this
process called celadon.

Their pottery, metalwork, and
carved jade pieces are known
as treasures around the world.
Koreans also made many
important discoveries and
clever inventions.

| | |
|---|---|
| 700s A.D. | Koreans carved page-sized woodblocks for printing books. Printing with blocks was much faster than writing by hand. |
| 1234 A.D. | Korean printers invented "movable type." They carved many small blocks. Each block printed one word and was moved from place to place, over and over, to print many different messages. |
| 1403 A.D. | Korean printers made the world's first metal movable type. They cast metal blocks in the same way that they cast metal coins. Cast-metal type is easier to make and longer lasting than wooden-block type. |

A statue of
King Sejong the Great

Once, all Korean writing
was based on Chinese
writing. It had thousands of
picture words and was very
hard to learn. But, in 1443,
King Sejong the Great told

The Korean alphabet is called *hangul*.

Korean scholars to invent a new Korean alphabet. They did.

*Hangul* is an alphabet with a written letter for every sound in spoken Korean. *Hangul* is easy to write and read and learn.

King Sejong believed in learning, for himself and for all Koreans. He studied time and he studied the stars and planets. While he was king, Koreans invented and used the sundial and a water clock. They also made maps of the solar system. They even invented ways to measure daily rainfall and to write and read music.

# THE HERMIT KINGDOM

A person who stays away
from other people is known
as a hermit. In the middle of
the 1800s, the kingdom of
Korea tried to stay away
from the rest of the world.
But the other countries
would not leave Korea alone.
They called Korea the hermit
kingdom.

China, Japan, Russia,
France, Great Britain, and
the United States—all sent

In 1876 Korea sent an ambassador to Japan.

ships and soldiers, as well
as diplomats and traders to
force open the doors to
Korea. They all tried to take
over and to make Korea buy
things from them.

Contact with these other
countries brought new ideas

Japan's Prince Hirobumi Ito (center) poses with Korea's young crown prince (seated) in 1908. By 1910, Japan ruled Korea completely.

and more war to Korea. By 1910 Japan ruled the Korean people.

| | |
|---|---|
| 1894 | There was war between Japan and China. When China lost, Korea became an independent kingdom. |
| 1904 | There was war between Japan and Russia. Japan won and moved its army into Korea. |
| 1910 | Japan made Korea a part of Japan. There no longer was a kingdom of Korea. The Korean people had lost their country and their freedom |

# TWO KOREAS

In 1945, Japan lost World War II, and the Japanese had to leave Korea. Still, Korea was not free. The Russian army took over the northern half of Korea. The United States army took over the southern half. Each wanted to keep the other country from taking complete control of Korea. The Koreans wanted their country back.

At last, the United Nations called for a Korean election. The United States agreed, but the Russians said no. Korea was split into two parts. The Russians set up a Communist government in North Korea. In 1948, South Korea held an election, adopted a Constitution, and formed its own government.

# THE KOREAN WAR

Then, in 1950, North Korea attacked South Korea. The United Nations sent a sixteen-nation army to help South Korea. Most of the soldiers were from the

U.S. troops attack a North Korean bunker. The Korean War was fought from 1950 to 1953.

The United States and the United Nations troops supported South Korea. Russian (above) and Chinese soldiers supported North Korea.

United States. Russia and China sent soldiers to help North Korea.

During the war, hundreds of thousands of soldiers and civilians were killed or wounded. Many of Korea's cities and towns were destroyed.

It seemed that the war

A frightened boy cries for help standing in the ruins of his home in Seoul, South Korea.

would never end. Finally, in 1953, an agreement was signed that ended the fighting. But the two sides are still separated. Today, a line divides the two Koreas. Soldiers are on guard on both sides of the line.

# NORTH KOREA

North Korea's capital city is Pyongyang. The Communist party controls the government.

In North Korea people work hard. They grow food, build new housing, and make products to sell to other Communist countries. Changes are slow to come, but the workers do have more food and better

A North Korean soldier

The Cultural Palace in Pyongyang, the capital city of North Korea.

housing than they had
before the war. The people
of North Korea are proud
of what they have done
since the war.

Seoul, the capital of South Korea, is a modern city. Toksu-Kung Palace (below) stands as a reminder of Korea's rich tradition.

# SOUTH KOREA

The capital and largest
city of South Korea is Seoul.
In South Korea everything
is busy, modern, and changing.
The people have improved
on what they have learned
from the rest of the world.

Seoul is home to more
than eight million people.

Classes are held to teach young Koreans traditional ways.

Today, most South Koreans wear modern clothes for work and play. Yet, as modern as they are, people still respect their families and the old Korean ways. Many Koreans wear traditional clothes on special holidays and family days.

A family celebration (above) in the city of Taegu

Although most Koreans wear Western clothes, it is not unusual to see traditional clothes (right) on the streets of Seoul.

High-rise apartments (above) and smaller houses and apartments (right) in Seoul

In towns and cities, most South Koreans live in houses or high-rise apartment buildings. In rural areas there are still some traditional Korean houses. They are made with clay,

Traditional Korean homes (left) and a modern solar home (right)

brick, or cement walls and
have thatch or tile roofs.
Stone pipes, called *ondol*,
are buried under the floors.
The pipes carry heat from
the kitchen fires to the rest
of the house.

35

Korean meals include soup as well as rice dishes. Cabbage
(right) often is used with a red pepper paste to make kimchi.

Korean food is very spicy. It is served at a low table in the main living room. Some of the favorite dishes are grilled meats, fish soup, lightly cooked fresh vegetables, and *kimchi*, a traditional pickled-vegetable dish.

# EDUCATION IN KOREA

Once, only the children of kings and powerful leaders were taught to read and write. For hundreds of years, education was used to keep families in power.

Today in Korea, education is for all the people.

Korean families place a high value on education for their children.

In North Korea, children must go to school for eleven years. Special training is given to adults.

In South Korea, children go to free primary school for

six years. Classes meet Monday through Friday, with a half day on Saturday.

After primary school, graduates may go to middle school, grades 7 to 9, but they must pay to attend. Middle school students study English as well as other subjects.

After middle school, some students go to special schools for job training. Others go on to high school.

High school students study Korean, English, and a third language, such as Japanese, German, French, or Chinese.

In high school, grades 10 to 12, students study such subjects as languages, history, mathematics, and science.

After high school, students either work in business or go on to college. South Korea has more than two hundred colleges or universities.

Seoul National University campus (left) and a high school chemistry class (right)

South Korean adults also
go to school to learn new
skills. As a result, more than
90% of South Koreans can
read and write. South Korea
has one of the highest levels
of learning in all the world.

# KOREA TODAY

South Korea's well-educated people make automobiles, television sets, microwave ovens, and computers. These products sell all over the world because they are well made.

On assembly lines, workers build video circuit boards (left) and automobiles (right).

The 1988 Summer Olympics were held at Seoul's Sports Complex (right). Tae kwon do was one of the featured sports.

In 1988 South Korea hosted the 24th Summer Olympic Games. Athletes from 161 countries competed. The South Korean people proudly showed their beautiful country and their busy way of life to the world.

43

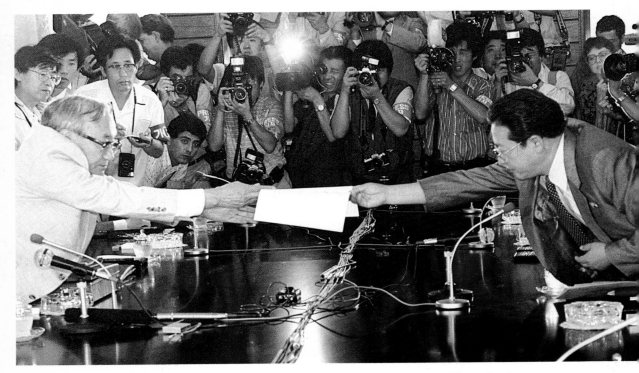

North and South Korean delegates met at Panmunjom before the Olympic Games.

North Korea would not
compete in the Olympics.
But, just before the games,
there were meetings
between North and South.
Maybe there will be more

Chang Dok Kung Palace in Seoul

meetings. Many Koreans
hope that the two parts of
Korea can find a way to stop
being enemies. Then, real
peace will come to the Land
of the Morning Calm.

# WORDS YOU SHOULD KNOW

**Asia**(AYJ • ah) — the largest continent on earth

**capital**(KAP • ih • tul) — the place where a country's government is located

**cast**(KAST) — poured into a mold, or form, and left to harden into the shape of the mold

**civilian**(sih • VILL • yun) — a person not in the military

**code**(KOHD) — a system of symbols used to send messages

**Communist**(KAHM • yoo • nist) — having a system of government under which businesses are owned by the state

**Constitution**(kahn • stih • TOO • shun) — a system of basic laws or rules for the government of a country

**diplomat**(DIH • pluh • mat) — a person representing a government to foreign countries

**election**(ee • LEK • shun) — the process of voting for or against a candidate or idea

**enemies**(EN • ih • meez) — dangerous, unfriendly persons or nations

**hangul**(han • GOOL) — the Korean alphabet

**hermit**(HER • mit) — a person who stays away from others

**humid**(HYOO • mid) — damp, moist

**inactive**(in • AK • tihv) — not active, not operating

**jade**(JAYD) — a green, white, or blue semiprecious stone

**kimchi**(kim • CHEE) — a Korean pickled-vegetable dish

**Olympic Games**(oh • LIM • pik  GAYMZ) — meetings held every four years, at which athletes from all over the world compete for prizes

**peninsula**(pen • IN • soo • la) — a piece of land almost surrounded by water and connected to a larger body of land

**Pyongyang**(PYONG • yang) — the capital of North Korea

**respect**(re • SPEKT) — honor shown to others; good treatment

**rural**(ROO • rul) — in the country

**scholar**(SKAH • ler) — a student with expert knowledge

**Seoul**(SOLE) — the capital of South Korea

**solar system**(SOHL • er SISS • tim) — the sun and its family of objects

**strait**(STRAYT) — a narrow water passage connecting two large bodies of water

**sundial**(SUN • dyel) — a shadow-casting device for telling time by sunlight

**tae kwon do**(tye kwan DOH) — a Korean martial arts sport

**technical**(TEHK • nih • kil) — having to do with science and mechanics

**traditional**(truh • DISH • in • il) — following a custom

**volcano**(vol • KAY • noh) — an opening in the earth's crust through which molten lava erupts

# INDEX

*About the Author*

*Karen Jacobsen is a graduate of the University of Connecticut and Syracuse University. She has been a teacher and is a writer. She likes to find out about interesting subjects and then write about them.*